I dedicate this little book to my loved ones who always support me and my wild ideas. Thank you for your love and for being my foundation.

Introduction

Disruption in business is often seen through the lens of cutting-edge technology and early adopters. However, this book takes a different perspective, focusing on the often underestimated yet pivotal role of the late majority in market disruption. This segment, traditionally viewed as slow to adopt new innovations, holds the key to sustained market acceptance and success. In the chapters that follow, we will explore how targeting the late majority can lead to a more profound and enduring form of market disruption, challenging conventional wisdom and offering a new paradigm for businesses looking to innovate and grow.

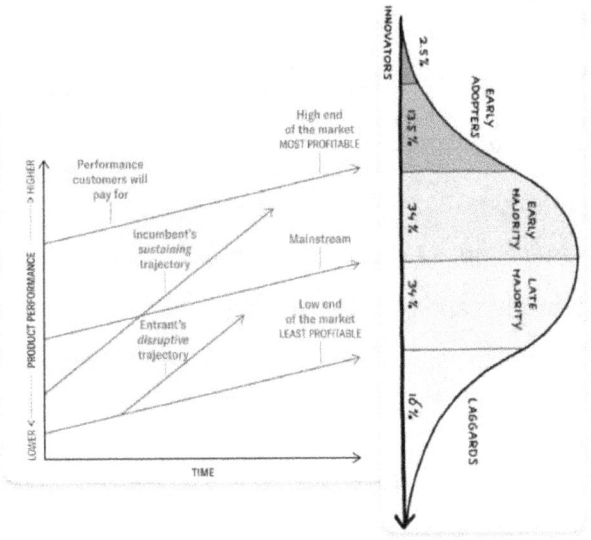

Culmination of the Disruptive Innovation Model by Clayton Christensen and Everett Rogers' Diffusion of Innovations.

The model above juxtaposes two significant concepts in innovation and market strategy: the Disruptive Innovation Model by Clayton Christensen and Everett Rogers' Diffusion of Innovations. The left side illustrates a disruption model, where a new entrant in the market begins by targeting the lower end of the market spectrum, gradually advancing to meet mainstream market needs. This trajectory contrasts with the incumbent's approach, which focuses on sustaining innovations at the higher end of the market.

The right side depicts Rogers' Diffusion of Innovation curve, segmenting the market into various adopter categories: Innovators, Early Adopters, Early Majority, Late Majority, and Laggards. This curve is instrumental in understanding how different market segments respond to new products or technologies over time.

The image, therefore, visually communicates the essence of the book's thesis: the potential of market disruption beginning with or significantly involving the late majority, a concept traditionally overlooked in disruption theory. It sets the stage for the detailed exploration in Chapter 1 of whom the late majority are, their characteristics, behaviors, and the potential untapped opportunities they present for sustained market disruption.

Time for a Metaphor...

In the realm of warfare, one of the most daring and strategic maneuvers is the deployment of troops behind enemy lines. These specialized units, often working under the cover of darkness and with limited support, are tasked with a critical mission: to disrupt the enemy's operations from within, paving the way for the main forces to advance. This approach, while risky, can be incredibly effective, catching the enemy off guard and causing disarray in their ranks.

This military strategy serves as a powerful metaphor for the concept of Lean Disruption, particularly in the context of targeting the Late Majority in the market. Traditionally, businesses have followed a linear path of innovation adoption, starting with the Innovators, moving to the Early Adopters, and then hoping to bridge the chasm to reach the Early and Late Majority. However, this approach often encounters significant challenges, akin to a frontal assault on well-prepared defenses.

Lean Disruption, much like the deployment of troops behind enemy lines, flips this traditional approach on its head. Instead of starting with the Early Adopters and fighting to cross the chasm, it targets the Late Majority directly. This is akin to infiltrating the 'enemy territory' – the larger, more established market segments that are often neglected by disruptive innovations.

By focusing on the Late Majority from the outset, Lean Disruption aims to create a stronghold within this segment. The Minimum Disruptable Products (MDPs) are designed to meet the specific needs and preferences of this group, which values practicality, reliability, and value for money over cutting-edge features. This approach can be more effective because it addresses a market segment that is typically less saturated and has more unmet needs.

Furthermore, just as troops behind enemy lines cause confusion and disarray, targeting the Late Majority can disrupt the market in unexpected ways. Incumbent companies, often focused on competing at the higher end of the market, may find themselves outflanked by products that cater to a different set of customer needs.

This can lead to a reordering of market dynamics, as the Late Majority, a segment usually seen as slow to adopt new technologies, becomes the driving force behind the adoption of the new innovation.

In conclusion, Lean Disruption, like a well-executed military operation behind enemy lines, challenges the conventional pathways of market entry and innovation adoption. By targeting the Late Majority first, it seeks to establish a foothold in an often overlooked but substantial market segment, disrupting the status quo and potentially leading to a significant reshaping of the market landscape.

Chapter 1: Understanding the Late Majority

Introduction to the Late Majority

Imagine a vast, untapped market segment, cautious yet sizeable, often overlooked yet holding the keys to widespread market adoption. This is the 'late majority' – the group that represents a critical threshold in the diffusion of new products and innovations. The late majority are not the trailblazers or the early birds; they are the deliberate and pragmatic individuals who wait to see proof before jumping on the bandwagon.

Behavioral Traits of the Late Majority

The late majority exhibit unique behaviors that set them apart. They prefer to stick to what's familiar, seeking comfort in the status quo until the balance of proof and practicality tilts. They are driven by practical needs and a desire for reliability, often seeking endorsements from their extensive social circles before making a commitment to something new.

Motivations and Drivers

What then shifts the late majority from a state of caution to one of acceptance? It's a combination of seeing widespread usage, the ironing out of initial technological kinks, the emergence of clear benefits, and the assurance of support and maintenance. For them, the adoption of innovation is not a leap of faith but a considered step towards improvement.

Barriers to Adoption

Several barriers stand tall in the path of the late majority's adoption of innovation. From a lack of understanding to an innate resistance to change, these barriers are not insurmountable but require strategic engagement. Education, simplified technology, and visible endorsement can each play a role in lowering these barriers.

The Role of the Late Majority in the Market

The late majority are the linchpin in the lifecycle of any product. Their buy-in often marks a transition from a niche product to a mainstream staple. They represent stability in the product lifecycle, a point at which the market settles, and a product becomes a part of the regular fabric of life.

Late Majority vs. Laggards

While both the late majority and laggards are late to adopt, they differ fundamentally. The late majority are cautious yet open to persuasion; laggards, on the other hand, are often unyielding, bound by tradition or simply disengaged from the technological zeitgeist.

Conclusion

To overlook the late majority is to miss out on a crucial element of the market adoption narrative. They are the bridge between a fringe innovation and a societal norm. As we turn the page to the next chapter, we will explore how traditional disruption models have underestimated the late majority, and why a new approach could reshape our understanding of market innovation.

Chapter 2: Traditional Disruption Models

Introduction to Disruption

Disruption has become a buzzword, synonymous with staggering innovation and market upheaval. It is the David versus Goliath of the business world, where the unlikely underdog emerges victorious. This chapter unpacks the traditional disruption model, laying the groundwork to understand where the late majority fits into this narrative.

Sustaining vs. Disruptive Innovation

At the heart of the disruption conversation are two distinct paths of innovation. Sustaining innovations represent the incremental improvements that companies make to their existing products to attract high-end customers willing to pay more. In contrast, disruptive innovations don't initially aim for the performance demanded by mainstream customers but offer other advantages, often affordability and accessibility.

The Dilemma of Incumbents

Established companies face the innovator's dilemma: by optimizing their products for their most demanding customers, they overlook simpler, more affordable alternatives. This myopia can create strategic blind spots, leaving incumbents vulnerable to more agile, disruptive entrants who can capitalize on ignored market segments.

Disruption from Below

The classic disruption narrative sees new entrants attacking the market from below. They target overlooked segments, often offering less sophisticated but more accessible products. Over time, these products improve, moving steadily upmarket and eventually satisfying the needs of the mainstream customer, by which point incumbents struggle to respond.

Early Adopters and Market Creation

The lore of innovation has always celebrated early adopters, those visionary enough to embrace new products and technologies before the rest become aware. They are the proving ground, the first dominos in the chain reaction of market acceptance, helping to validate the disruptor's proposition.

Limitations of Traditional Models

Yet, this traditional model may not tell the whole story. It assumes a linear path of adoption and a one-size-fits-all strategy for market entry and expansion. It underestimates the complex dynamics of market segments, particularly the late majority, who are often relegated to the role of passive bystanders in the saga of disruption.

Conclusion

As we close this chapter, we recognize the strengths of the traditional disruption model but also its gaps. We pave the way for a new perspective, one that sees the late majority not as an afterthought but as a potential catalyst for innovation. The next chapter will delve into this uncharted territory, exploring how the late majority could be the cornerstone of a new disruption paradigm.

Chapter 3: The Case for Late Majority Disruption

Introduction: Challenging the Status Quo

In the tapestry of market innovation, the late majority has often been a forgotten thread. This chapter re-examines their role, proposing that they are not merely followers but pivotal players in sustaining market disruption.

Revisiting the Adoption Curve

The late majority, forming a substantial part of the consumer base, wields significant market influence. Their eventual endorsement is crucial for an innovation to achieve enduring success.

Success Stories: Late Majority Led Disruptions

- Uber's Transportation Revolution: Initially appealing to tech enthusiasts, Uber's real triumph was in swaying the late majority. Their transition to this convenient, app-based service marked a seismic shift in urban transportation habits.

- Amazon's Retail Evolution: Amazon began as an online bookstore, capturing the interest of early adopters. However, it was the late majority's gradual acceptance of online shopping that transformed Amazon into a retail titan, reshaping the entire retail landscape.
- Netflix and the Streaming Era: Netflix, starting with DVD rentals, moved to streaming, initially a novelty for many. The late majority's adoption of this service revolutionized media consumption, making digital streaming the norm.

Late Majority as a Market Force

Far from being laggards, the late majority represents a bridge to widespread market acceptance. Their cautious approach to adoption, once seen as a barrier, is now understood as a pathway to stable and sustainable market growth.

Strategic Advantages in Targeting the Late Majority

Targeting the late majority offers strategic advantages, such as reduced competition and the potential for long-term customer loyalty. Engaging this segment can lead to robust and resilient business models.

Psychology of Late Majority Adoption

Understanding the late majority's psyche—grounded in pragmatism, social proof, and value assessment—is key to crafting innovations that resonate with their values and needs.

Conclusion: A New Paradigm for Disruption

In conclusion, this chapter repositions the late majority from passive adopters to active shapers of market disruption. It lays the groundwork for the following chapter, which will delve into specific strategies for effectively engaging with this influential market segment.

Chapter 4: Strategies for Engaging the Late Majority

Introduction: Understanding the Audience

To effectively engage the late majority, a deep understanding of their characteristics is essential. This chapter outlines strategies tailored to resonate with this pragmatic and cautious segment.

Building Trust with the Late Majority

Trust is paramount in appealing to the late majority. Techniques like showcasing user testimonials, emphasizing product reliability, and focusing on long-term benefits are crucial. The power of word-of-mouth and social proof, especially among peer groups and trusted networks, plays a significant role in influencing their choices.

Simplicity and Accessibility

Simplicity in both product design and marketing messaging is key to winning over the late majority. Products with user-friendly interfaces and marketing materials free from technical jargon help demystify new technologies, making them more accessible and less intimidating.

Affordability and Value Proposition

The late majority seeks value for money, making affordability a significant factor. Strategies that balance cost-effectiveness with a strong value proposition, perhaps through tiered pricing models or demonstrating long-term savings, can be particularly effective.

Gradual Introduction of Innovation

A phased approach to innovation, introducing new features progressively while anchoring them in familiar functionalities, can help mitigate the late majority's resistance to abrupt change. This strategy allows for a smoother transition and better acceptance.

Utilizing Influencers within the Late Majority

Engaging with influencers within the late majority community, such as respected local figures or community leaders, can lend credibility and relatability to the innovation. These influencers can act as advocates, making the new product more appealing to the late majority.

Effective Communication Channels

Identifying and leveraging the right communication channels is critical. For the late majority, traditional media channels, community-based events, and direct communication methods like newsletters or direct mail might be more effective than purely digital campaigns.

Feedback Mechanisms and Continuous Improvement

Establishing feedback channels and demonstrating a commitment to continuous improvement based on this feedback can reinforce trust and loyalty among the late majority. This approach shows a dedication to meeting their specific needs and concerns.

Conclusion: A Comprehensive Approach

In conclusion, engaging the late majority requires a multifaceted strategy that builds trust, ensures simplicity and accessibility, offers value, and communicates effectively. The next chapter will delve into real-world examples where these strategies have been successfully implemented.

Chapter 5: Case Studies of Engaging the Late Majority

Introduction: Real-World Examples

This chapter presents real-world case studies that illustrate effective strategies for engaging the late majority, offering insights into how various industries have successfully navigated this challenge.

Case Study 1: Transition to LED Lighting

The shift from incandescent to LED lighting is a prime example. Manufacturers and retailers focused on the long-term cost savings and environmental benefits of LEDs, while ensuring the bulbs maintained a familiar appearance. Educational campaigns highlighting the longevity and efficiency of LEDs helped to ease the late majority's transition to this new technology.

Case Study 2: Mobile Banking Adoption

Banks faced significant challenges in introducing mobile banking to the late majority. Strategies included developing user-friendly interfaces, offering extensive customer support, and ensuring robust security measures. Banks also used traditional advertising channels to communicate the convenience and benefits of mobile banking, gradually building trust among the late majority.

Case Study 3: Health and Fitness Wearables

The adoption of health and fitness wearables by the late majority was facilitated by emphasizing ease of use, affordability, and the tangible benefits of health monitoring. Influencer marketing, especially by figures relatable to the late majority demographic, played a significant role in increasing acceptance.

Case Study 4: Online Grocery Shopping

The COVID-19 pandemic accelerated the adoption of online grocery shopping, including among the late majority. Key to this shift was the emphasis on the convenience and safety of remote shopping. Retailers ensured that their online platforms mirrored familiar in-store experiences, easing the transition for late majority shoppers.

Effective Strategies Summary

These case studies highlight the importance of a gradual approach, an emphasis on value and simplicity, and the effective use of familiar communication channels and influencers in engaging the late majority.

Conclusion: Lessons Learned

These examples provide valuable lessons in engaging the late majority. By understanding their preferences and resistance points, and employing targeted strategies, it's possible to successfully transition this critical market segment to new innovations and technologies.

Chapter 6: The Path to Mainstream Adoption

Introduction: From Late Majority to Market Norm

The transformation of an innovation from a niche product to a mainstream staple is a journey marked by significant milestones, one of which is the late majority's adoption. This segment, often overlooked, serves as a key indicator of a product's readiness for widespread market acceptance. Their endorsement often marks the turning point for an innovation's market success.

The Role of Late Majority in Market Dynamics

The late majority, with their preference for tried-and-tested products, play a pivotal role in stabilizing market trends. Their adoption of an innovation is not just an increase in sales numbers; it represents a shift in market perception and consumer trust. This transition is critical for establishing a product's long-term market presence.

Case Study 1: Electric Vehicles

Electric Vehicles (EVs) have evolved from being an ecological novelty to a mainstream choice. Key to this shift was the late majority's gradual acceptance, influenced by advancements in battery technology, increased charging infrastructure, and government incentives making EVs more accessible and practical.

Case Study 2: Telemedicine Services

The telemedicine industry saw an unprecedented boost during the pandemic. The late majority's adoption was driven by necessity but sustained through the realization of its convenience and effectiveness. Policies facilitating telemedicine and technological enhancements played a significant role in this adoption, showcasing how external factors can accelerate market acceptance.

Case Study 3: Smart Home Technologies

Smart home technologies initially appealed to tech enthusiasts but have since seen broader acceptance. The late majority's adoption was facilitated by user-friendly interfaces, enhanced security features, and the ability to integrate with existing home systems, making the technology less intimidating and more appealing.

Overcoming Market Saturation Challenges

Once a product reaches mainstream status, maintaining innovation becomes a challenge. Strategies like targeting niche markets, continuous product improvement, and diversification help keep the product relevant and appealing in a saturated market.

Feedback and Continuous Evolution

Feedback from the late majority is invaluable for continuous product evolution. Their insights can lead to meaningful improvements, ensuring that the product remains relevant and meets evolving consumer needs.

Conclusion: Sustaining Innovation in a Mature Market

In summary, the journey to mainstream acceptance is complex and multifaceted, with the late majority playing a crucial role. Understanding their needs and preferences, and continuously evolving based on their feedback, is key to sustaining innovation in a market where a product or service has become the norm.

Chapter 7: Risks and Considerations in Targeting the Late Majority

Introduction to strategic risk

While targeting the late majority offers unique opportunities for market penetration, it's crucial to be aware of the inherent risks and considerations. This chapter delves into these challenges, highlighting the importance of a strategic and balanced approach.

Market Complacency Risk

Focusing predominantly on the late majority could lead to market complacency. This risk involves becoming too comfortable with current success and failing to innovate, potentially missing out on future market shifts or technological advancements.

Misalignment with Early Adopters

Targeting the late majority might alienate early adopters and innovators, who are typically the first to try new products. Maintaining their interest is crucial for initial market traction and continuous feedback, essential for product refinement.

Pace of Technological Change

The rapid pace of technological change presents a significant challenge. Innovations may evolve faster than the late majority's adoption rate, leading to a mismatch between product offerings and consumer readiness.

Balancing Product Evolution

Striking a balance in product evolution to cater to both early adopters and the late majority is complex. Products need to be sophisticated enough to interest early adopters while remaining accessible and appealing to the late majority.

Overdependence on a Single Market Segment

Relying heavily on the late majority for growth can be risky. Diversification across different market segments is crucial for sustainable business growth and reducing vulnerability to market changes.

Economic and Market Shifts

Economic downturns, technological breakthroughs, or shifts in consumer preferences can impact the late majority's behavior. Companies must remain adaptable and responsive to these changes to retain this segment's loyalty.

Conclusion

In conclusion, while the late majority is a critical market segment for sustained growth, solely focusing on them can be risky. A balanced and flexible approach, considering the needs and dynamics of all market segments, is vital for long-term success.

Chapter 8: Future of Disruption: Late Majority's Growing Influence

Introduction to the future of disruption

As we look towards the future of market disruption, it becomes increasingly important to understand the evolving role of the late majority. This chapter explores how emerging trends, technological advancements, and shifts in consumer behavior are likely to influence the late majority's impact on market dynamics.

Technological Advancements

Advances in technology (especially in AI, IoT, and mobile connectivity) are set to reshape the way the late majority interacts with new products and services. These technologies could make innovations more accessible and appealing to this segment, thus accelerating their adoption rates.

Changing Consumer Behaviors

Global trends such as increased environmental consciousness, the rise of remote work, and demographic shifts are likely to influence the late majority's purchasing decisions. We might see a greater emphasis on sustainability, convenience, and affordability that will dictate the direction of future market disruptions.

Market Evolution

Market dynamics are expected to shift significantly. The late majority's role in validating and sustaining new products will become even more crucial. Companies might start to design products with the late majority in mind from the outset, rather than treating them as an afterthought.

Innovative Strategies

In response to these changes, innovative strategies will emerge. We might see more companies adopting a 'late majority first' approach, focusing on reliability, ease of use, and value for money right from the product development phase.

Conclusion

The late majority's growing influence in market disruption is undeniable. As we move forward, the key to sustained market success will lie in understanding and adapting to their evolving needs and preferences. Companies that can effectively engage with this segment while balancing the needs of other market segments are likely to thrive in the future of market disruption.

Chapter 9: The 'Job-to-be-Done' in MDP Design

Introduction: The Job-to-be-Done

In the journey of crafting a Minimum Disruptable Product (MDP), grasping the concept of the 'job-to-be-done' is paramount. This chapter uses a metaphor from a simple hardware store scenario to unravel this crucial framework, setting a foundation for understanding customer needs beyond their immediate requests.

The Hardware Store Metaphor

Picture a bustling hardware store on a sunny afternoon. A customer walks in, looking slightly bewildered amidst aisles of tools. They approach the assistant, asking for a hammer. The assistant, seasoned and knowledgeable, leads them to a wall displaying hammers of all shapes and sizes. From claw hammers to sledgehammers, each one is suited for different tasks. The assistant starts suggesting the feature filled hammer trying to convince the customer to buy the new and fancy hammers. On each occasion the customer seems unsatisfied with the suggestion. Frustration builds until the assistant pauses and asks, "What do you need the hammer for?"

The customer explains they're setting up a campsite and need to drive tent pegs into the ground. In a moment of realization, the assistant realizes that all the customer want is a simple rubber mallet - the perfect tool for the job. This interaction illuminates the essence of understanding the underlying task or 'job-to-be-done.' The important question that needs to be asked is not about the tool, but about the task at hand.

Deep Dive into 'Job-to-be-Done'

The 'job-to-be-done' theory, a concept developed in the business and marketing world, fundamentally shifts focus from the product to the customer's underlying need. It was popularized by Clayton Christensen, who argued that customers 'hire' products to get a job done. At its core, this approach is about empathy and understanding - seeing beyond the product's features to the actual outcomes that customers seek.

This concept goes beyond superficial customer requests, probing into the underlying reasons for those requests.

It's not about the product itself but about the progress a customer seeks to make in a particular circumstance. For instance, when buying a coffee, the job might not be about drinking coffee per se, but about finding a quick energy boost, a warm comforting break, or even a space for informal meetings.

In the hardware store metaphor, the customer didn't need just any hammer; they needed a solution to set up their campsite efficiently. The job wasn't hammering; it was about hassle-free camping. Understanding the job-to-be-done allows companies to innovate more effectively. It's about solving the right problems and addressing unmet needs.

This framework has been successfully applied across various industries, from consumer electronics to healthcare, often leading to breakthrough innovations. It challenges businesses to think from the outside in, starting with the customer experience and working backward to the product.

In summary, the 'job-to-be-done' framework encourages a deeper understanding of customer needs, focusing on the task they seek to accomplish. This understanding is crucial for developing products that genuinely resonate with users, particularly in the context of creating an MDP for the late majority.

The Nuance of Customer Needs

The key to understanding the late majority lies in perceptive listening and keen observation. Often, their needs are not explicitly stated but implied in their lifestyle, preferences, and pain points. This involves engaging in deeper conversations, conducting user studies, and empathetic observation to uncover their real challenges and aspirations.

Consider a company that developed gardening tools for elderly users. Initially focusing on functionality, they later realized their customers valued tools that were easier to handle and less strenuous, aligning with their physical comfort needs.

Another example is a tech company that, after observing that their older users were intimidated by complex interfaces, simplified their product design. This not only made their products more accessible to the late majority but also enhanced overall user experience.

In essence, understanding customer needs, especially for the late majority, requires a blend of empathy, observation, and a willingness to look beyond the obvious. It's about connecting with their experiences and genuinely addressing the 'job' they need to accomplish.

Applying the Framework to MDP

To effectively apply the 'job-to-be-done' framework to an MDP, start by identifying the core task the late majority seeks to accomplish. This might involve extensive market research, direct customer interviews, or ethnographic studies.

The design process of the MDP should then be centred around these findings, ensuring that every feature and function directly contributes to accomplishing the identified job. It's about simplicity and utility, stripping away anything that doesn't serve the primary purpose.

One common pitfall is assuming the needs of the late majority without proper validation. Avoid this by continuously engaging with the target audience throughout the development process.

Another risk is overcomplication. Remember, the MDP should remain lean and focused. Adding too many features too soon can dilute its effectiveness and appeal to the late majority.

Finally, be wary of misinterpreting feedback. Ensure that the feedback collection and analysis process is thorough and objective, providing a clear picture of the late majority's needs.

In summary, applying the 'job-to-be-done' framework to MDP requires a deep understanding of the late majority's core needs, a focused approach in product development, and vigilance against common development pitfalls.

Conclusion

The 'job-to-be-done' framework is more than a tool; it's a mindset that focuses on the customer's true goal. Understanding this concept is crucial for developing an MDP that resonates with its intended audience, especially when that audience is the late majority. This chapter is not just about tools and products; it's about uncovering and addressing the real tasks at hand.

Chapter 10: Crafting a MDP for the Late Majority

Introduction: The MDP

Introducing the concept of a Minimum Disruptable Product (MDP) as a novel strategy in market disruption, this chapter emphasizes targeting the late majority. By aligning a product with the specific 'jobs-to-be-done' of this segment, businesses can initiate a more profound market transformation.

Understanding the Late Majority

A deep dive into the late majority's characteristics reveals a cautious yet sizable market segment. Their decision-making processes, driven by reliability and value, set the foundation for MDP design.

Designing the MDP

Key considerations in creating an MDP involve simplicity, reliability, and affordability. The product must not only meet the functional requirements of the late majority but also align with their comfort level and value perception.

Iterative Development and Feedback

The development of an MDP is an iterative process, heavily reliant on feedback from the late majority. Strategies for engaging with this group and incorporating their input are discussed.

Marketing and Communication for MDP

Effective marketing strategies for MDPs are outlined, focusing on clear messaging, and leveraging channels that have high resonance with the late majority, like traditional media and community-based platforms.

Conclusion

Concluding the chapter, the potential of a well-designed MDP to disrupt the market by appealing to the late majority is underscored. This approach marks a shift in traditional disruption strategies, opening new avenues for market impact.

Chapter 11: Bridging the Gap by Enticing Early Adopters with Enhanced MDP Features

Introduction: Reverse Adoption

This chapter explores the unconventional strategy of adapting a Minimum Disruptable Product (MDP), initially designed for the late majority, to attract early adopters. This reverse approach challenges the traditional innovation adoption model and presents unique opportunities for market disruption.

The Unconventional Journey: Late Majority to Early Adopters

Traditionally, innovations target early adopters first, gradually moving to the late majority. However, this chapter discusses the reverse path: starting with a product tailored for the late majority and then enhancing it to appeal to early adopters.

Understanding Early Adopters

Early adopters are characterized by their willingness to embrace new technologies and trends. Unlike the late majority, they are attracted to innovations offering uniqueness, advanced features, and a sense of exclusivity.

Enhancing the MDP for Early Adoption

The key lies in adding features that align with early adopters' desires without alienating the late majority. This could include integrating advanced technology, offering customization, and incorporating a design that signifies innovation.

Case Studies: Successful Transition from Late Majority to Early Adopters

- Dropbox: Starting in a competitive market with no clear demand, Dropbox created an MVP and showcased its utility through a simple video. This initial presentation was crucial in validating customer interest, drawing thousands to their beta. Continuous improvement based on user feedback led to significant growth, with the company eventually valued at over $12 billion.

- Slack: Initially an internal tool for a gaming startup, Slack pivoted towards a broader market following feedback from external users. This feedback loop was instrumental in evolving Slack into a powerful communication tool, appealing to larger organizations and leading to a user base of over eight million and a successful IPO.

Marketing and Communication Strategies for Early Adopters

The marketing for these enhanced products shifts focus, highlighting aspects like innovation, exclusivity, and technological superiority. This shift is crucial in rebranding the product to attract early adopters.

Conclusion

This reverse approach of targeting early adopters after establishing a market presence with the late majority offers a fresh perspective in the landscape of market disruption. It underscores the potential of a flexible, adaptive product strategy in navigating different market segments.

Conclusion: Embracing the Late Majority in a Disruptive Future

In conclusion, this exploration into the role of the late majority in market disruption has revealed a landscape ripe with opportunities and challenges. The journey from niche innovations to mainstream acceptance hinges significantly on this segment. The late majority, once seen as reluctant adopters, emerge as crucial players in validating and sustaining market changes. As we move forward, businesses must adopt a more inclusive approach, considering the diverse needs and behaviors across all market segments. Embracing the late majority not as an afterthought but as a central strategy could be the key to enduring success in an ever-evolving market landscape.

The goal of this book, if you can call it that, is to plant a seed and provoke thought, enticing business geeks to build on this theory by developing revolutionary approaches to market disruption.